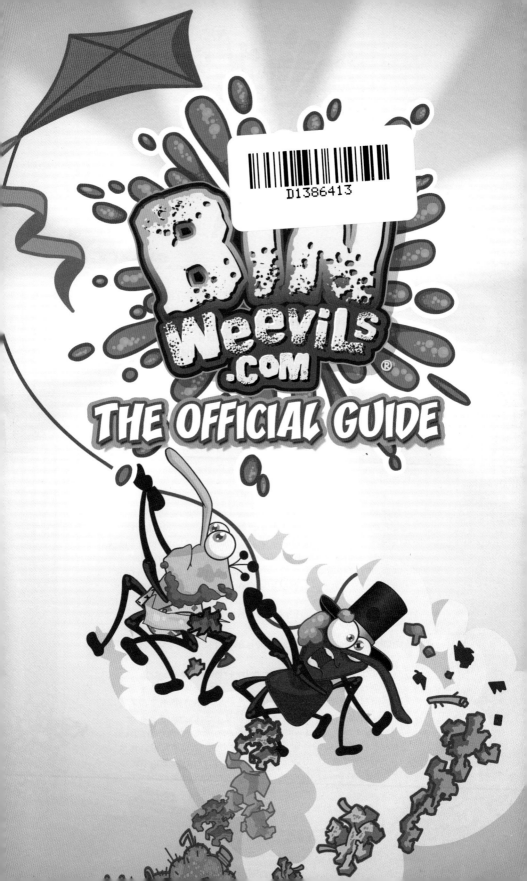

BIN Weevils .COM®
THE OFFICIAL GUIDE

First published 2011 by Macmillan Children's Books
a division of Macmillan Publishers Limited
20 New Wharf Road, London N1 9RR
Basingstoke and Oxford
Associated companies throughout the world
www.panmacmillan.com

ISBN 978-1-4472-0006-2

Written by William Petty

1 3 5 7 9 8 6 4 2

A CIP catalogue record for this book is available from the British Library.

Printed and bound in Italy by Printer Trento s.r.l.

CONTENTS

INTRODUCTION

Do you want to explore an amazing online world that's full of ever-changing fun? From the moment you create your unique Bin Weevil character, you'll be on a Bin-tastic journey filled with adventures, missions, challenges and games. Find your friends online and make tons of new buddies too as you meet all the wacky inhabitants of the Bin! Challenge your pals to games, solve fiendish puzzles and enter competitions to win brilliant prizes. Every day, you can explore a changing Binscape, unlock hidden secrets and put your wits to the test!

Together with your friends, you can watch the latest TV shows whenever you want, and even read extracts from cool new books. It won't be long before you're invited to incredible online parties, meeting the Bin's celebrities and picking up exclusive items for your Bin Nest. Your nest is your home within the Bin, which you can expand, decorate and customize to make it your very own. Shop for the perfect items, deck out your rooms and invite your buddies to come and check it out!

Your Bin Weevils adventure is waiting for you . . . so fall in and flip out!

This book will tell you everything you need to know about the Binscape.

With this book in hand, you'll be ready to explore and discover all the amazing things Bin Weevils has in store! You'll have the ultimate info right at your fingertips to make the most of your weevily experience.

Along the way you'll meet the characters, learn cool new secrets and pick up top tips to get ahead in the world of Bin Weevils! By the time you get to the end of the book, you'll be a certified Bin Weevils expert.

GOLDEN CROWNS
Be on the lookout for the Golden Crowns hidden throughout the book. Find them all and write down what pages you found them on, in order from the first page to the last. The numbers form a secret code that you can use to unlock a special nest item in the Mystery Code Machine in front of Lab's Lab!

The hidden Golden Crowns look exactly like this. Count this one first, then find five more!

ITEM CODE:

7 ___ ___ ___ ___ ___

Find the remaining five crowns to win a cool nest item!

Best moment: Coming up with his latest & greatest plan!

TINK

If there's something crazy going on in the Bin, Tink's usually behind it! Never a day goes by without Tink coming up with a new harebrained scheme to earn Mulch. His plans almost always go wrong, but when you think you're a genius, you don't get put off easily – you think on your feet and come up with a new, equally loopy idea! With his best buddy Clott by his side, Tink is always happy to help the other residents of the Bin – whether they want him to or not!

Quote:

'I've got an idea!'

Greatest ambition:
To put on an amazing Bin Carnival!

CLOTT

Clott is Tink's ever loyal, long-suffering best friend. These Boys from the Binscape are next-door neighbours, and they're always together, usually because Clott has been roped into another one of Tink's mad plans. Clott will do whatever he can to help out his friend, even when a more sensible Bin Weevil would have walked away. But that's what makes Clott such a useful partner – he doesn't do a lot of thinking! He's always trying to come up with ways to impress Posh, mostly with disastrous results.

Best moment:

Helping Tink in his mad plans.

Greatest ambition:
To impress Posh!

STAYING SAFE ONLINE

Follow these simple guidelines to help keep Bin Weevils a safe, friendly place to hang out!

• Never give out your real name. When you sign up to Bin Weevils, you will choose a unique Bin Weevil name – this is how other people on the site will know you, and you will be able to recognize your buddies by their Bin Weevil names.

• Never share your personal information. Don't tell other users where you live, how old you are, or where you go to school. You shouldn't ask others for this information either – don't ask anyone to tell you their real name, address, phone number, email address or password.

• Don't use bad language. Never swear or use words that other people might find offensive or unkind. Bullying and mean behaviour are not allowed!

• Don't put up with bad behaviour. If someone says something to upset you on the site, you can add them to your Ignore list, which means they won't be able to talk to you. Or you can report them to the site moderators, who will decide what to do.

• Play fair and don't cheat!

PASSWORD SAFETY

A good password is something that's easy for you to remember, but very hard for anyone else to guess! Never use your real name or any part of your Bin Weevil name as a password. It's a great idea to use a silly random word, or even a word you made up! Using a number in your password is another smart idea.

Never share passwords with anyone except a parent. If you share your password with someone else, they could log in to your account, spend all your Mulch and turn your nest upside down! You wouldn't give anybody the key to your front door, so don't give other users your password.

Never ask your friends to share their password with you, either – passwords are private!

If you think somebody else might know your password, change it as soon as you can by using the link underneath the login area.

NOW YOU'RE READY TO CREATE A BIN WEEVIL!
To do this, click on GET STARTED! on
the login page!

GET STARTED!

FREE!

CONTROLS

Congratulations, you are now a Bin Weevil! Let's start off by having a look at the controls that let you interact with the Binscape!

LEVEL

This tells you what level your Bin Weevil has achieved, and how many Experience Points (or XP) you still need to reach the next level. The more you play, the higher your level goes, and the more cool items you'll be able to buy in the Shopping Mall! You'll also unlock new missions, special moves and activities as you level up.

MULCH

This is the Bin Weevils' currency, which you use to buy things. This indicator tells you how much Mulch you have. You can earn Mulch by playing games, completing hunts and missions, harvesting your Bin Garden and more!

How do I get more XP? You can earn XP in loads of ways, including playing games, buying items, getting your nest rated, harvesting your garden and taking part in missions.

How can I get more Mulch? If you're a Bin Tycoon member, you can earn more Mulch by opening a Bin Tycoon business or starting your own magazine!

FOOD

If your food bar is getting low, find a restaurant or a cafe and grab a snack! If your Bin Weevil is hungry, it will make a funny face.

FITNESS

Your fitness level will go up as you do special moves and actions. The fitter you are, the more actions you will be able to do before your Bin Weevil gets tired.

HAPPINESS

Playing games, watching TV shows, doing puzzles and rating other Bin Weevils' nests will top up your Bin Weevil's happiness. Keeping your happiness high will make your plants grow faster!

MAP

The Map shows all the locations in the Bin and lets you get from place to place in the blink of an eye! You can always click on your nest in the bottom left corner of the map to get back home instantly.

TOP TIP
Play the Daily Brain Strain at Lab's Lab every day to earn lots of XP and Mulch.

MY STUFF BOX

This is where any items you find or buy will be stored. Click on it to see what's inside, then click on it again to close it.

ACTIONS MENU

Click here to see all the actions (special moves) that your Bin Weevil has unlocked so far. You can also use keys 1–5 for some moves.

MAKING FRIENDS

CHAT BAR
This is what you use to talk to other Bin Weevils. Type in what you want to say and press return or click on the 'send' button.

CHAT LOG
Click here to look back on recent conversations.

BUDDY LIST
This is a list of all your weevily friends. When another user asks to be your buddy, an envelope will pop up from here. Click on it to review your buddy invitations and accept new buddies.

IGNORE LIST
See a list of any Bin Weevils you have chosen to ignore.

NEST INVITATIONS
This is a list of all your invitations to visit other Bin Weevils' nests. Click on the envelope to see your list of invitations and pick which nest to go to first!

GUEST LIST
See and edit a list of the Bin Weevils you've invited to your nest!

MESSAGE INDICATOR
This symbol will let you know how many new buddy requests and nest invitations you have.

PROFILE BOX
Click on a Bin Weevil and their profile box will pop up.

 Send a buddy request to this Bin Weevil.

 Invite this Bin Weevil to your nest.

 Ignore this Bin Weevil (this means they can't talk to you).

Report this Bin Weevil to a moderator.

If the Bin Weevil is already on your buddy list, the buttons will be slightly different:

 Find this buddy if they are online, or check when they last logged in if they are offline.

 Remove this buddy from your buddy list.

 Send a message to this buddy.

 If this buddy is currently on your ignore list, click here to take them off.

Bin Buddies

Scribbles
Gene
Tevil
Bubbabin
TheWeeble
larrynoname
Kennwenny

SPECIAL TYCOON CONTROLS!

Go straight to Tycoon TV Towers.

Take a picture of you and your friends at any time!

TOP TIP
Buddies who are online right now in the same Bin as you will appear in dark letters.

BECOME A BIN TYCOON

Join the upper crust of Bin Weevil society!

Expand your nest & garden – Tycoons can have up to ten rooms in their nests!

Buy cool hats – Headgear is the mark of a stylish Bin Weevil. Collect dozens of different hats!

WELCOME TYCOON ISLAND

SLIME POOL

Visit Tycoon Island –
This playground of the rich and fabulous is only open to Bin Tycoons.

Own your own businesses –
Open your own Tycoon Plaza for business, and outfit glittering nightclubs and a chic photographic studio.

Create your own magazine –
You're the editor-in-chief, and you decide what the whole Bin simply has to know about!

Adopt a Bin Pet –
Train and take care of your little friend, bring it with you for walks, and watch it do tricks to impress your buddies!

17

WELCOME TO YOUR NEST

TOP TIP
Agent Clott holds the secret to finding the Secret Weevil Service

GARDEN

GARDEN PIPE
Click here to step outside into your Bin Garden. Turn to page 24 to find out more about gardens!

MYSTERY PORTAL
Not sure what to do next? Go through this door to be transported to a random place in the Bin. Adventure awaits you!

NEST ROOMS
Each Bin Weevil starts with one room, so only one door will be open. But that can all change as you start expanding your nest to unlock up to ten rooms!

MAILBOX
If you get sent a direct message by one of your buddies, it will show up in here. Your mailbox will flash to let you know you've got mail!

NEST NEWS!

TYCOON FAIR UPDATE!

COLOUR SLIDER
Adjust the colour in your nest's entrance hall!

Jojo's nest
NEST SCORE: 1246

NEST NEWS
If there's a party coming up, a hot new competition or exciting changes to the Bin Weevils' world, you can guarantee the story will be here first!

NEST SCORE
Your nest score goes up whenever other users rate your nest.
To learn more, turn the page!

Bin Tycoon!

FUEL-O-METER
The more stuff you have in your nest, the more fuel you need to keep your lights on and your gadgets powered up. Click on the Fuel-o-Meter to keep your fuel topped up regularly, or you could find your nest plunged into darkness – and what sort of impression is that going to make on your guests?

How do I get another room for my nest?
To buy a new nest room, visit Rigg's Property Shop on the top floor of the Shopping Mall!

DECORATE YOUR NEST

The MY STUFF box holds all your nest items. Whenever you buy an item from a shop, claim a prize from a party, collect a fan poster or earn a trophy, all your stuff will appear in here.

DECORATING

To place an item in your nest, click on the treasure chest icon to open the MY STUFF box, then click and drag the items you want into your nest room. You will have to open up the MY STUFF box whenever you want to move items around inside your nest rooms or move items in and out of your nest.

ROOM RATING

Whenever you invite someone to your nest, they will be able to rate your rooms. This score is shown in your nest hall. Good ratings will earn you more XP, so you'll want to impress them.

ORNAMENTS

Some items, like trophies, can only be placed on shelves and tabletops, so you will need to buy some before you can show off your awards!

TOP TIP

Visiting another Bin Weevil's nest means you can rate their rooms, and rating their rooms will boost your Happiness!

The MY STUFF box only shows you items that can be placed in the room in which you're standing. If you've bought items for a business or seeds for your garden, you will need to move to the correct location before you'll see those items in your box.

NOT DELIVERED YET

BEST NESTS

With the right combination of items and accessories, you can build a brilliant nest room! You can even win a Bin Nest Trophy if your design impresses the Nest Inspector. To learn more about the Nest Inspector and to read some cool tips on decorating your nest, see page 34.

The bathroom

My living room

The kitchen

23

YOUR BIN GARDEN

Planting and harvesting your Bin Garden is one of the fastest and best ways of earning Mulch and XP. Purchase some seeds from the Garden Shop, plant them in your garden and watch them grow into zany, wacky and wonderful flowers, mushrooms, trees and more! When they're ready, you can harvest them to earn your reward.

Some plants will wither and die after a certain time, so make sure you check on them regularly and harvest them while you can. Other plants remain in your garden forever and can be harvested over and over again. Permanent plants and statues can be moved around your garden to give it a brand-new look.

BUY SEEDS

To buy a watering can, and more seeds, you'll need to visit the Garden Shop. It's in the Shopping Mall, but there's a shortcut to get there from your garden – just click on the sign that says BUY SEEDS.

To water a plant, first place your watering can anywhere in your garden. Then click on the plant you want to care for. If the plant can be watered, you will see WATER as an option in its mini menu.

TOP TIP
If a plant looks a little sad and dull, it needs to be watered.

CLICK . . . IF YOU DARE! Clicking on a plant will tell you how close it is to being fully grown or ready to harvest. But some plants also animate when you click. Yeow! This Venus Flytrap is vicious!

TOP TIP
The Death Cap Mushroom costs more Mulch to buy than you will get back for harvesting it. Sounds like a crazy deal at first, until you notice that it packs a whopping 40 XP when harvested! If you have Mulch to spare and want to level up quickly, this mushroom is ideal!

DID YOU KNOW?
Your garden path takes you straight to FLUM'S FOUNTAIN!

TOP TIP
Start planting at the very edge of your garden, as close to your nest as you can. Plant around the border first and then work your way towards the middle, placing your plants as close together as possible to maximize your gardening space.

TOP TIP
Go green! Some garden items, like this windmill, can generate power for your nest and save you Mulch!

ACCESSORIZE! Not everything in your garden is of the growing variety — colourful fences, silly scarecrows, or even an outhouse can give your garden some real personality.

MEET THE BIN WEEVILS

THE GARDEN INSPECTOR

Quote:

'Go green!'

The Garden Inspector loves being surrounded by greenery. She is seldom found indoors, and prefers to spend most of her time hopping from garden to garden, awarding trophies for the best ones she sees. The Garden Inspector firmly believes that plants need music to thrive, so she sings opera to them at every opportunity. She's been known to sleep outside in her lawn chair so the plants don't get lonely at night!

Best moment: Discovering the magical powers of the Giant Beanstalk seed.

Greatest ambition:
           To collect one of every rare seed.

AROUND THE BINSCAPE

This is your Bin Nest. Click here whenever you want to return home.

This is the Binscape! As far as the eye can see, there are cool places to visit, tricky missions to complete and lots of games to play. The Binscape is always changing, so explore, explore, explore and you never know what you might find!

You can always click on an area of the Map to jump there quickly, but you can also check the map to see how the areas are linked together if you want to walk around using the connecting paths.

DOSH'S PALACE

MULCH SHOOT

PLAY GAME ←

Dosh's Palace is elegant and sophisticated in every way. Magnificent fish-head fountains spew forth delightful torrents of dirty water either side of its imposing facade. This place just oozes luxury!

TOP SECRET!

Click on all the rubies on the side of Dosh's Palace and prepare to be amazed!

MEET THE BIN WEEVILS

DOSH

Dosh is the richest Bin Weevil – he's absolutely rolling in Mulch! He's always been minted, and he just can't understand why everyone isn't as rich as he is. He spends his time swanning around the most glamorous spots in the Bin, spending Mulch like there's no tomorrow. When Dosh isn't spending his lovely loot, he's cleaning it – he loves his Mulch to be spotless, and he's got fifteen washing machines to get all the dirt out!

Best moment:

Earning his first million Mulch.

Greatest ambition:
To build the tallest stack of Mulch ever recorded.

THE BIN WEEVIL CHANGER

Inside Dosh's Palace, you'll find the amazing Bin Weevil Changer machine. Here, you can choose the shape and colour of your head, eyes, body, legs and antennae. When you find a look you're happy with, save it and exit!

If you're bored with your look, you can pop back into Dosh's Palace any time and give your Bin Weevil a full makeover! From the shape of your body to the colour of your antennae, for just a small amount of Mulch you can give your Bin Weevil a whole new style.

CHANGE THE WAY YOUR BIN WEEVIL LOOKS HERE!

BIN WEEVIL CHANGER ⓘ

DID YOU KNOW?
There are over six billion possible combinations, so you'll never run out of unique Bin Weevil looks to try out!

If you're very lucky, Dosh himself might appear in the Palace! If you see Dosh come out on to his balcony, get your clicking fingers ready, because he's been known to shower Mulch down on the grateful Bin Weevils below!

TOP TIP
Want to attract attention and draw a crowd? Visit Dosh's Palace with some buddies and change your colours to match each other! Everyone will stop and stare when they see a big group of lime green Bin Weevils hanging out at Flum's Fountain!

MEET THE BIN WEEVILS

THE NEST INSPECTOR

The Nest Inspector is a very special Bin Weevil. His job is to wander the Binscape to find the best nest in town! When he finds a nest that is absolutely BIN-tastic, he awards the owner an exclusive Bin Nest Trophy either in bronze, silver or gold. These trophies are not sold in shops – the only way to get your weevily fingers on one of them is to find the Nest Inspector and invite him to your nest! The Nest Inspector loves his job, but he also loves his holidays, and can often be found sipping on a cold smoothie at the beach.

Best moment: Discovering a trophy-winning nest!

Greatest ambition: To design the bestselling nest item of all time.

HOW DO I GET A BIN NEST TROPHY?

If you see the Nest Inspector, send him an invitation to visit your nest. You can be sure that it's really him because his Bin Weevil name is NEST_INSPECTOR, and when you click on him a unique profile picture will pop up that looks like this:

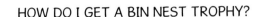

NEST_INSPECTOR

The Nest Inspector also has his very own magazine, BEST NEST. The magazine is packed full of decorating tips and images of the best nests in the Binscape. You can read BEST NEST inside Weevil Post, at Rigg's Multiplex.

NEST CHECKLIST

All rooms fully decorated! ✔   Fill up your shelves! ✔

Themed rooms are fab! ✔   Don't forget the flooring! ✔

Lighting brightens things up! ✔   Collections are cool! ✔

THE SHOPPING MALL

If you've got some Mulch burning a hole in your pocket, visit the Shopping Mall for some retail therapy. Everything you could possibly want is on sale here, from brilliant themed wallpaper to insane gadgets and golden toilets!

DID YOU KNOW? If you can't find what you're looking for, come back soon! Items for sale in the shops change every twenty minutes, so it's never the same shopping trip twice!

FLEM

Quote:
'SNIFFFF!'

Flem has a perpetual cold, and when he doesn't have a cold, he has hay fever! Sniffle, snort, snuffle, sniff, that's how you know when Flem's around. Still, he doesn't let the sniffles get him down and he's always busy ordering in the latest designer nest items for his Furniture Shop. That, and getting through a whole lorry-load of tissues!

Best moment:

The time he went a whole hour without sneezing.

Greatest ambition:

To expand his manor and overtake Dosh's Palace in luxury.

THE FURNITURE SHOP

Fancy seating for true superstars!

Fluffy comfort with a dash of cuteness!

Zoom straight into dreamland!

W3Y1L2

MEET THE BIN WEEVILS

ZING

Quote:

'Zowie!'

Greatest ambition: To memorize every word that begins with the letter Z.

Zing is a zany Bin Weevil who's always zooming around with zest. She absolutely can't stay still for more than an instant, which is why her favourite gadgets are the ones that never stop moving! From robots to rocket ships, you'll always find the perfect gadget or gizmo in Zing's shop. The only thing she loves more than gadgets is the letter Z.

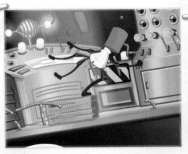

Best moment: Seeing Lab's top-secret super laser plans!

GADGETS & GIZMOS

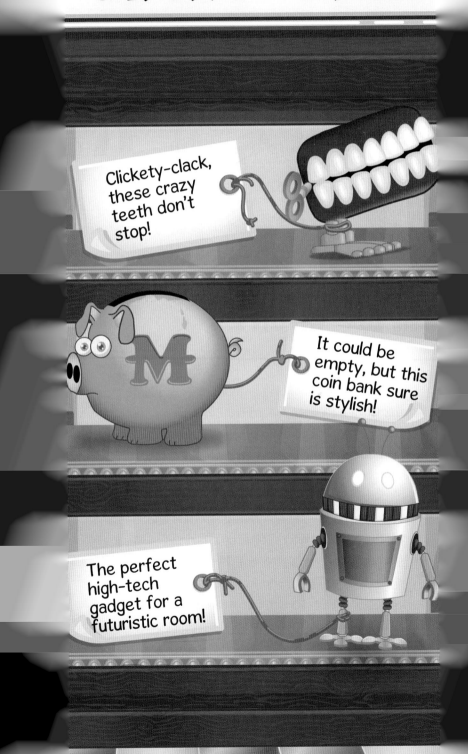

EXIT

£0000

GRUNT

Quote:
[a series of excitable grunting sounds]

BIN WEEVILS
BIN WEEVILS

Grunt is a true plumbing enthusiast. He's won the Golden Plunger Award for Bin Weevils Services to Toilets every year as long as anyone can remember – although we don't think anyone else enters! It's no surprise that his shop is the Kitchens & Bathrooms Shop, offering the latest and greatest in tubs and toilets, sinks, furniture, tiles, countertops, kitchen stools and more. His favourite item is the Golden Toilet, and though he hates to part with one every time he makes a sale, he assures its new owner that if it ever needs repair, he's their Bin Weevil!

Best moment:
Winning the Golden Plunger Award, of course!

Greatest ambition:
To rework all the leaky plumbing in Gam's Castle!

42

KITCHENS & BATHROOMS

FAB

Fab loves everything and everyone –
you won't find a nicer Bin Weevil
anywhere in the Binscape. Everything
in Fab's world is sunshine and rainbows
and butterflies and . . . well, it's just
fab! She loves paging through BEST
NEST magazine to see where all the
floors and wallpapers she's sold have
ended up. Fab's seen it all when it
comes to interior decorating, but when
she visited Clott's place, imagine her
surprise to find that he had
wallpapered the ceiling and installed a
window on the floor!

Greatest ambition:
To cheer everyone up!

Quote:

'What a beautiful Bin day – isn't it fab?'

Best moment:
Designing a custom-made carpet for Dosh's Palace.

TAB

If there was a world championship in worrying, Tab would take gold, silver and bronze. He worries from the moment he wakes up in the morning until the moment he falls asleep (which sometimes isn't until he's spent a whole night lying awake worrying). When Bin Weevils come into his shop, he worries. When no Bin Weevils come into his shop, he worries! Basically, Tab worries a lot.

Quote:
'Be careful!'

Greatest ambition:
To have nothing to worry about apart from the fact that he has nothing to worry about!

THE GARDEN SHOP

Sometimes wishes really do come true . . .

It goes down in flames and comes back more beautiful!

The shining jewel in any Bin Tycoon's garden!

RIGG

Quote:

'I built that!' (Even when he didn't!)

Best moment:

When he sacked Tink and Clott.

Rigg is a big character in the Binscape. He thinks big, he acts big, he's got a big head and a big heart. He's also into building big buildings – his construction projects are everywhere, and he's always got a plan for what to build next. Sometimes his big imagination makes him say he built something even when he didn't, but nobody minds. He once hired Tink and Clott to work on his building site. That was a BIG mistake!

Greatest ambition:

To build a suspension bridge to Mulch Island.

RIGG'S PROPERTY SHOP

At Rigg's Property Shop, you can expand your nest by purchasing extra nest rooms! If you're running out of space to display all those cool nest items, trophies and posters, it's time to branch out and invest in some weevily real estate! Remember, the more rooms you have, the faster your nest score and XP will accumulate! You can find Rigg's Property Shop on the top floor of the Shopping Mall.

To buy more space for your nest, choose a room from the floor plans.

NEST FLOOR PLANS

BIN PETS

Bin Pets are loads of fun, and training them is an exciting challenge! If you're ready to adopt a pet, you can find the Bin Pet Shop in the Shopping Mall.

The first thing to do when you get your pet back to your nest is to place its bowl and basket in one of the rooms.

(i) Your pet lives in your nest – whenever you log out of Bin Weevils, your pet will climb into the basket and go to sleep. It will be waiting for you when you return, eager to play!

XP: Learning and performing tricks increases your pet's XP.

Energy: Moving around and doing tricks will tire out your pet, and its energy bar will go down. If your pet's energy is low, it needs to rest.

Food: This bar goes down when your pet is hungry. When it gets to red, your pet needs food urgently! Try to feed your pet when the bar is orange.

Health: If your pet has had too much or too little to eat, or gets unfit or tired, its health bar will go down. But some good care will bring it back to good health quickly!

Fitness: Doing lots of actions will make your pet fitter.

Orange

XP: 10356

ENERGY
FOOD
HEALTH
FITNESS

DON'T PANIC!
If you can't remember what to do, don't worry. This button on your pet profile will take you straight to the Bin Pet Guide!

TOP TIP
Reward your pet when it learns something new. Hold the mouse over your pet for a few seconds to give it a stroke – this will make it learn faster.

PET TRAINING

There are three types of skills your pet can learn:

General skills
Your pet learns to listen to commands such as 'stay' and 'sit'.

Orange

XP: 10356

ENERGY
FOOD
HEALTH
FITNESS

Ball skills
Pets can be trained to fetch and throw balls, or even juggle!

Spinning skills
Your pet can perform a variety of acrobatic twists and spins.

It's important to keep your pet happy and healthy – it will tell you if something is wrong. If your pet starts to get tired, it will need to go to bed and rest. Don't wake it up until its energy levels have gone up, or it will just go back to sleep again.

When your pet gets hungry, click on the bowl to give it some food. Make sure you don't overfeed it though – your pet will eat whatever you give it, and too much food is unhealthy! Pet Mulch can also be purchased at the Bin Pet Shop.

DID YOU KNOW?
Bin Pets like to play with other Bin Pets! Try taking your pet outside for a walk and see how it acts when it meets another Bin Pet.

TOP TIP
Having trouble getting your Bin Pet to jump on your back? Before asking your pet to 'jump on', make sure you are standing right next to it or he/she will not be able to reach you.

CLUB FLING

CLUB FLING

It's all happening here at the coolest club in the Binscape! Outside, see if you can get the party started with some giant party blowers. Then step inside to show off your funkiest moves on the dance floor, before spinning some tunes on the decks. Or head upstairs to the chill-out zone, where you can relax on the comfy cushions, grab a snack or play a game with friends. Outside on the roof you'll find more games, and the Bin's biggest confetti cannon!

DID YOU KNOW? Bin Tycoons can work together to unleash some extra XP! Three Bin Weevils will need to stand on the three white lights over the entrance. Stay put, and watch the tube opposite fill with a strange purple goo. When the goo reaches the top, it'll explode in a shower of bubbles, filling the air with valuable XP to collect! Click on it quickly before it disappears!

Fling's a Bin Weevil who can never stop dancing! Fling just couldn't understand why nightclubs have to close sometimes, so he decided to open his own club, and it NEVER closes! No matter what time of day or night, if you're in the mood to dance you will find the bright lights shining at Fling's!

INSIDE CLUB FLING

The dance floor inside Club Fling is a great place to show off your weevily moves. Doing special moves is not only fun, it also keeps your Bin Weevil's fitness up!

DID YOU KNOW?
Clicking on the buttons beside the DJ booth will activate some awesome strobe light effects – perfect if you're taking a pic!

MEET THE BIN WEEVILS

FLING

Fling's got dancing fever, and he's got it bad! He likes his music loud and his feet moving. Most Bin Weevils can't work out what Fling's on about half the time, but luckily his funky moves speak for themselves. He's strutted his stuff all over the Bin, and he makes sure the hottest tunes are spinning at Club Fling, the Bin's must-visit dance spot.

Best moment:

Winning the Bin Weevils dance-off.

Greatest ambition:
To always win the Bin Weevils dance-off!

THE LOUNGE

KONNECT MULCH

Aim: To make a line of four of your colour Mulch Balls.

How to play: Take it in turns with your opponent to drop a Mulch Ball into the rack. It will fall all the way to the bottom. Use your Mulch to make a line of four, while trying to stop your opponent from getting four in a row.

TOP TIP
If you go first, drop your Mulch in the middle column – it will give you the best chance of winning!

TOP TIP
If you get your Mulch in one of the four corner squares, it's there to stay — your opponent won't be able to flip it back again.

FLIP MULCH

Aim: To end up with more of your colour Mulch on the board than your opponent.

How to play: Take turns putting a Mulch Ball on the board. Every time you make a line of Mulch with your colour at each end and your opponent's colour in the middle, all their Mulch flips over and becomes YOUR Mulch! But watch out — it could all flip back again next go!

TOP SECRET!
Jump on all the cushions in Fling's Lounge to discover a silly surprise!

THE POOL HALL

A world away from the glitz of Club Fling, the Pool Hall is where down-to-earth Bin Weevils like to come for a game of pool in gritty, grungy surroundings. The floor may be dirty, and the wallpaper may be peeling, but it feels like home!

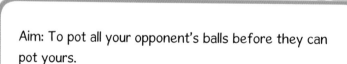

Aim: To pot all your opponent's balls before they can pot yours.

How to play: To hit one of your balls, click on it, drag back, and release. Choose the angle and power of each shot to knock the other player's balls into the pockets.

TOP TIP
If your balls end up near the edges of the table and far from the pockets, they will be harder to pot.

FLUM'S FOUNTAIN

Flum's Fountain is an awesome place to chat with buddies and get to know new Bin Weevils – it's where everyone stops to chill, and there's a reason it's named after the Bin's most famous reporter!

You can water the mushrooms to make them grow! To do this, you'll need to make the Fountain spray jets of water in their direction.

To set off a jet of water, jump on the lit-up blue pads that activate randomly around the border of the Fountain. Act quickly to jump on to a pad while it's still lit up!

TOP TIP
If you've interviewed somebody for your mag, ask them to join you at Flum's Fountain for a pic. Zoom right in on them to get the perfect front-cover snap!

FREE CAM

While you're hanging out with your pals, try using the Free Cam to look at the world in a different way. Not only can you get a clearer view of the growing mushrooms, but you can also move the camera in close to see your own Bin Weevil or a buddy in more detail. Wow!

By clicking the different buttons and sliders on the Free Cam, you can look around 360 degrees. Use the zoom slider if you want to take a closer peek at something.

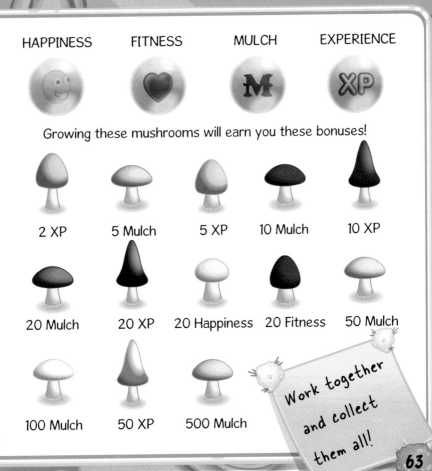

HAPPINESS   FITNESS   MULCH   EXPERIENCE

Growing these mushrooms will earn you these bonuses!

2 XP   5 Mulch   5 XP   10 Mulch   10 XP

20 Mulch   20 XP   20 Happiness   20 Fitness   50 Mulch

100 Mulch   50 XP   500 Mulch

Work together and collect them all!

RIGG'S MOVIE MULTIPLEX

It's always showtime at Rigg's place! The Multiplex is Rigg's pride and joy, his greatest achievement to date. There were some memorable moments while it was being built, many of them not so pleasant for Rigg . . . You can bet that whenever Tink and Clott are involved, there are bound to be a few disasters! However, the structure finally went up and this famous Bin cinema is now a haven for celebrities and cool Bin Weevils alike. It's a great place to watch top shows from the best kids' TV networks. You can even catch up on the madcap antics of Tink and Clott in the Bin Weevils cartoons!

New Bin Tycoons will want to swing by the cash machine outside Weevil Post and pick up their cool Bonus Mulch. Tycoons will also find their earnings from their businesses here!

DID YOU KNOW? You can read magazines written by other Bin Weevils by clicking on the news stand. A random selection of mags will be listed each time. If you want to read a specific Bin Weevil's mag, click on him or her and select the magazine icon from their profile box.

FIGG'S CAFE

If your tummy is rumbling, head to Figg's Cafe for some yummy grub. There's always something delicious on the menu to fill you up. Or why not help out by serving food to hungry Bin Weevils? They're sure to thank you!

Can you help Figg unjumble her menu? Check your answers on page 158!

MENU

CONES

HOUNDGUT

CHINWADS

EMUSOS

MURGENIE

Step in here to grab your copy of BEST NEST or WEEVIL WEEKLY, two of the Bin's most popular mags!

Could you use a bit of extra Mulch? Of course you could! So don't forget to swing by one of the three Mulch-Tastic Kiosks and pick up your daily free ticket! Create your own personalized ticket by scrolling through the symbols until you reckon you've found a lucky combination.

Every three days at 5 p.m., a lucky ticket will be picked, and if any of its symbols are in the same place as on your ticket, you're a Mulch winner! The more symbols that match the winning ticket, the more you'll get. Don't worry if your symbols don't come up – you can choose a new ticket every day.

TOP TIP

The Mulch draw happens every three days, but you can get four tickets for each draw if you're clever! Claim your first ticket on the day of the draw, right after the draw is finished. Then claim one on the next two days, and on the third day – the day of the next draw – pick one up before the draw takes place!

DIRT VALLEY

If you like to race, this is your place!
Prove you've got the sharpest driving
skills in the Bin as you take on one, two
or three other Bin Weevils in thrilling
races. There are three awesome 3D
tracks to master, all with different
difficulty levels.

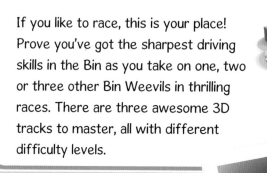

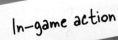

In-game action

GAME CONTROLS

fire active
weapon

Z
accelerate

X
turbo

steer
left

↑

← ↓ →

brake

steer
right

Before you race against others, do a few practice laps in the time trials. When you think you're ready, pick a car and wait for some challengers. You'll need to win a trophy on each track before you move on to the next one. If you're the day's top racer, you'll even get to see your name in lights over the track – and so will everyone else!

TOP TIP
You can use the turbo button (X) all the time, but be sure to release it when you need to get more grip on the corners.

BUBBLES - As you zoom around the track, pick up all the bubbles you can along the way to get cool items that you can use to slow down your competitors.

SLIME PAT – Drop this oily mess in front of another racer and they'll spin out! But be careful – you might hit it yourself on the next lap.

HOMING SPLAT – Beware of any racer with this yellow cloud above them. Don't get too close or it will home in on you!

STINK SHOT – Use this if you want to hit the racer in front of you.

TRACK 1

TRACK 2

TRACK 3

LAB'S LAB

The roof of Lab's Lab is bristling with sciency stuff for finding out about the world. Lab's is the home of all that is brainy and mind-boggling in the Bin, and this is the place to come for the Daily Brain Strain.

TOP SECRET!

Lab loves Crazy Eights! Click the 8-Ball on the top of Lab's Lab eight times and see one of Lab's tricks!

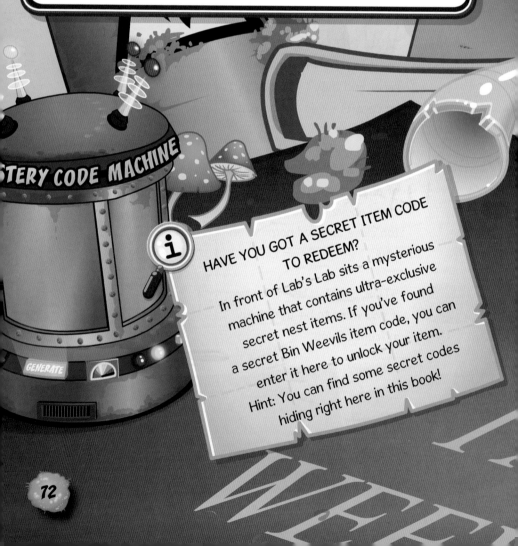

STERY CODE MACHINE

GENERATE

HAVE YOU GOT A SECRET ITEM CODE TO REDEEM?

In front of Lab's Lab sits a mysterious machine that contains ultra-exclusive secret nest items. If you've found a secret Bin Weevils item code, you can enter it here to unlock your item. Hint: You can find some secret codes hiding right here in this book!

THE DAILY BRAIN STRAIN

It's great to know things for their own sake, but if you're smart, you can turn your knowledge into cold hard Mulch and XP inside Lab's Lab! Lab asks the questions, and the more you answer, the more you'll win. Visit once a day to strain your brain – you won't regret it!

Study up for the Brain Strain with these practice questions. It's a race, so time how long you take to do them!

Hit the right button to turn on the light,

$$17 + ? = 31$$

- 12
- 14
- 19
- 15

Can you speak French?
What do these words mean in English?

Maison
- [ ] House
- [ ] Mouse

Chat
- [ ] Hat
- [ ] Cat

Pain
- [ ] Bread
- [ ] Head

How many Squares?

How many Circles?

How many Hexagons?

75

Flag Test!

Which country does this flag belong to?

Germany	Mexico
USA	Brazil

Time's Up!

Can you write the digital versions of these times?

LAB

Quote:

'I know the answer to that!'

Lab is the Bin's very own mad scientist. Well, he's not THAT mad compared to some of the other characters wandering the Binscape . . . but he sure is mad about knowing stuff! This brainbox knows nearly everything, which is why he can breeze through the Brain Strain without his bulging brain even breaking a sweat. He's full of fantastic facts that he's happy to share with the other Bin Weevils. He's also fascinated by Clott, because Clott looks at the world in a totally different way from anyone else. Well, he's sure got that right!

Greatest ambition: To know everything backwards.

Best moment: Unveiling his maddest creation at the Mad Scientist Party.

FLEM MANOR

There's always lots of creative stuff going on at Flem Manor – it's delightfully arty! Before you pop inside to soak up some weevily culture, make sure you have a crack at the Spot the Difference puzzles in the tent outside – wow, are they tough!

Spot
the
Difference

Once inside Flem Manor, sweep majestically up the grand staircase and hang a right to the library, where you can check out extracts from the coolest new books.

Spot

Flem Manor is also the place to be for word puzzles! Take a wander into the crossword and wordsearch room if you're low on Mulch. Each puzzle you complete will earn you a nice reward.

BTINKLSO
UPNSDDJK
NMKIPAOT
TUMRNETC
YCLOTTHY

Photo 1

SPOT THE DIFFERENCE!

Photo 2

Can you spot the ten differences?

79

WORD PUZZLES

Complete the puzzles to test your word skills!
The wordsearch words can be found horizontally, vertically and diagonally.

```
C O M P E T I T I O N P B L E
H R B I N S C A P E M A U E X
A A N T E N N A E I Q R D V P
L C S C Z T Y C O O N T D E E
L I T H V M Y S T E R Y I L R
E N U A D E C O R A T E E M I
N G D T E A S M U L C H S I E
G N I G H T C L U B W G P S N
E M O S E N H A R V E S T S C
B J T R W S H O P P I N G I E
N A C O I T E M S G T F O O D
H E R G A V U M A G A Z I N E
S C H A P P I N E S S M B S E
H U N T N Z V E F I T N E S S
M U L T I P L A Y E R Z I S P
```

J
C
W
T

ANTENNAE   EXPERIENCE   ITEMS   PARTY
BINSCAPE   FITNESS   LEVEL   RACING
BUDDIES   FOOD   MAGAZINE   SECRETS
CHALLENGE   GAMES   MISSIONS   SHOPPING
CHAT   HAPPINESS   MULCH   STUDIO
COMPETITION   HARVEST   MULTIPLAYER   TYCOON
CROWN   HATS   MYSTERY
DECORATE   HUNT   NIGHTCLUB

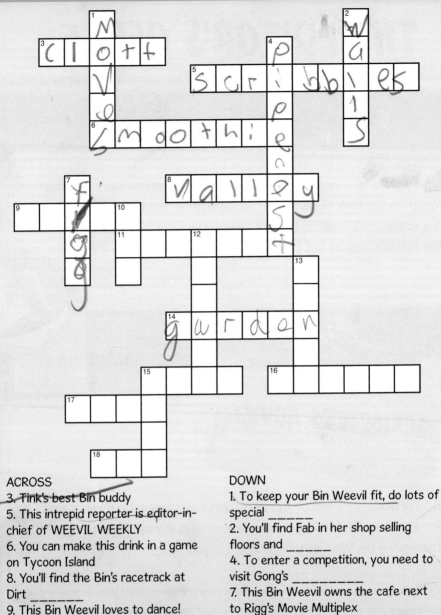

Crossword grid answers (handwritten):
- 3 Across: CLOTT
- 5 Across: SCRIBBLES
- 6 Across: SMOOTHIE
- 8 Across: VALLEY
- 14 Across: GARDEN
- 1 Down: MOVES
- 2 Down: WALLS
- 4 Down: POPPEACOST
- 7 Down: FIGG
- 12 Down (partial letters visible)

ACROSS
3. Tink's best Bin buddy
5. This intrepid reporter is editor-in-chief of WEEVIL WEEKLY
6. You can make this drink in a game on Tycoon Island
8. You'll find the Bin's racetrack at Dirt _____
9. This Bin Weevil loves to dance!
11. To get to Mulch Island, you'll have to catch a plane at Rum's _____
14. You can earn Mulch and XP by harvesting plants in your _____
15. This Bin Weevil is always sniffling!
16. If you impress the Nest Inspector, he might give you this
17. If your nest has gone dark, you'll have to buy more of this
18. This Bin Weevil sells hats on Tycoon Island

DOWN
1. To keep your Bin Weevil fit, do lots of special _____
2. You'll find Fab in her shop selling floors and _____
4. To enter a competition, you need to visit Gong's _____
7. This Bin Weevil owns the cafe next to Rigg's Movie Multiplex
10. The oldest Bin Weevil in the Bin
12. To change your Bin Weevil's look, you will have to enter Dosh's _____
13. The best Bin Burger is served at Tum's _____
15. Scribbles got his nickname because he loves to write, but his name is actually _____

THE EDITOR'S OFFICE

Bin Tycoons who want to publish their own magazines flock to Flem Manor to get their fingers inky. To the right of the hall, at the bottom of the stairs, you'll find the Editor's Office. Once you're inside, just click on the editor's desk to get started!

SCRIBBLES'S ADVICE:

1) Interviews are loads of fun to read! Hanging around in a social area like Flum's Fountain (my personal favourite) is a great place to find fascinating Bin Weevils to interview for your mag.

2) A picture always makes your story more interesting! When there's a new party or a new area in the Bin, weevil on over with your camera in tow to snap that perfect shot!

3) The more users who read and rate your mag, the more Mulch you'll earn! Other Bin Weevils can read your mag by clicking on you, so be online at busy times and mention your new mag to everyone you meet. If they've got a mag too, be sure to read and rate theirs in return!

TOP TIP
Pick something zippy,
zany and totally unique
for your magazine name
to help everybody
remember your mag!

83

SCRIBBLES

Scribbles's real name is Flum, but everyone knows him by his nickname. He's always been called Scribbles because he's seldom without a pen in his hand and he's always scribbling things down! He's the editor-in-chief of the popular WEEVIL WEEKLY magazine, and he's never happier than when he's roaming the Binscape, intrepidly chasing down an exclusive story to bring to his readers. If you see this roving reporter out and about, don't miss the opportunity to talk to him – he could make your name famous if he interviews you for his mag!

Best moment: The first publication of WEEVIL WEEKLY magazine.

Greatest ambition: To interview every Bin Weevil in the Bin.

INTERVIEW WITH SCRIBBLES

Scribbles is always on the move, interviewing Bin Weevils all over the Bin. But this time, the tables are turned! We asked what YOU wanted to know about our favourite reporter, and you sent in your questions for Scribbles! Here are some of Scribbles's answers.

carly57 –
What's your favourite place in the Bin?

You might think it's Flum's Fountain because it was named after me. But my favourite place is actually the Editor's Office inside Flem Manor, because that's where my WEEVIL WEEKLY magazine comes to life!

froggy2003 –
Where do you get all of your brilliant ideas from?

My fans, of course! I like to interview Bin Weevils and ask lots of questions.

reyi –
Scribbles, what does Bin Weevils mean to you?

Bin Weevils means everything to me! Without the Bin and my weevily fans, I would be lost!

27club -
Do you think all Bin Weevils are equal no matter what their experience and level?

Absolutely YES! You should only judge a Bin Weevil by their personality.

Winniem -
What first gave you the idea to make WEEVIL WEEKLY?

A long time ago I noticed that many Bin Weevils had a lot of great questions, opinions and ideas. I thought about how I could share what I saw and heard with every Bin Weevil. What better way to do this than to start up a weekly magazine!

tashatoucan -
What's your favourite crazy move?

I love to do several moves at the same time: jump, head shake and arms swinging in the air! Are you wondering how it is possible to do all three moves at once? It's simple – just try pressing the numbers 1, 2, 3, 4 on your keyboard really fast!

x-PurpleAngel-x -
Why do you like writing magazines?

My favourite thing of all time is writing WEEVIL WEEKLY magazine!
I love being a reporter because you get to play detective and try to
dig up interesting stories. When something happens in the Binscape
I also like to interview and hear other Bin Weevils' opinions. Being a
reporter allows me to meet interesting Bin Weevils every day –
that's why I love it so much!

princess-cutie1 -
What is your favourite game in the Bin?

My favourite game is the Brain Strain puzzles at Lab's Lab. I think
Lab did a great job in designing them. He is super smart and I like
that about him!

cali37 -
How do you feel with all the attention?

I like the attention. But sometimes there are lots of Bin Weevils
talking to me and I can't talk to everyone at once. My biggest
worry is coming across as rude! I try my weevily best to talk to
as many Bin Weevils as possible.

SLAM'S PARTY BOX

This box may not look like much from the outside, but it's been the site of many of the Bin's greatest ever parties. Don't be downhearted if you find it closed — you can't party here every day, but there'll be something crazy going on soon.

Easter Party

TOP TIP
The WHAT'S NEW blog is a great place to find out about upcoming events in the Bin and parties at the Party Box!

Check out these legendary past shindigs at the Party Box. There will be plenty more parties to come!

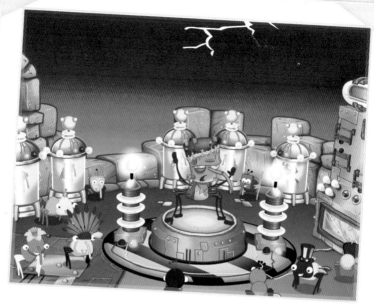

Mad Scientist Party

UFO Party

Make sure you don't miss a Bin party! They last for several days, and you can pick up unique items to decorate your nest at each one. But once it's over, it's over!

CASTLE GAM

TOP SECRET!

Castle Gam is full of mysteries! Clicking on a certain brick on the outside of Castle Gam might reveal one of them to you . . .

Castle Ga

TOP TIP
Whenever you draw the third side of a square, your opponent can draw the fourth side and claim the square as their own – so always avoid drawing the third side!

SQUARES

Aim: To make more squares than your opponent.

How to play: Take it in turns with your opponent to connect two dots with a line. When you complete a square by drawing its fourth side, the square becomes yours – so make a square whenever you can! Every time you complete a square, you get another go. You can complete long chains of squares this way.

MEET THE BIN WEEVILS

GAM

The glory days of this old soldier are long past, but that doesn't stop him reliving his proudest moments. Give him half a chance, and he'll take half a day telling you about the swashbuckling adventures of his youth. Just make sure you shout your approval, as he's a bit hard of hearing these days. His home, Castle Gam, is as old as he is, although it only just survived one of Tink and Clott's loony schemes. Pull up a stool, and Gam will tell you all about that, too. Battling pirates and zombies is easy as pie compared to the antics those two can get up to . . .

Best moment:

Becoming the chief of the SWS.

Gam in his glory days!

Greatest ambition: To write his action-packed autobiography.

THE SECRET WEEVIL SERVICE

TOP SECRET

TOP SECRET
Report

Ref No.
DC/FI Bin Section

Special Agents Tink and Clott

AGENT TINK

AGENT CLOTT

SECRET WEEVIL SERVICE
SWS

Once you've gained access to Gam's castle, you will find yourself at the heart of the SWS headquarters. If you are ready to serve your fellow Bin Weevils and join the elite ranks of those who have sworn to protect the Bin, then accept the challenge and enlist in SWS missions here! You'll gain Mulch and XP for successfully completing missions, but take note: only the bravest Bin Weevils need apply!

SWS MISSIONS

TROUBLE AT CASTLE GAM!

Your first SWS mission is to save Castle Gam from being flooded with slime! Find your way through the maze to reach the control room and help Rigg fix the pipes before it's too late!

You'll have to negotiate your passage with Gam's guards, solve riddles and puzzles, and explore the dark dungeon with nothing more than a torch for light. It's definitely not for the faint-hearted Bin Weevil, but the rewards are great if you keep your wits about you.

The Entrance

The Pipe Room

The Cavern

SECRET CODE

SWS Agents, we've just received a top-secret code! Hold this page up to a mirror to reveal the code, then enter it in the Mystery Code Machine at Lab's Lab to unlock some free bonus Mulch!

SWS9ꟼꓘⱭꓘ⅃ႲꟼꓘⱭꓘℲ

TOP TIP
Did you know that there are dozens of Mulch coins just lying around in the Castle Gam dungeons? Even if you've already explored an area, you can always come back to search for Mulch!

Think you're a good shot? Look carefully at these balls of flying Mulch, then close your eyes and draw a cross with a pen where you think each one is. How many did you get?

5

LEVEL

A fast-paced game for the sharp-eyed Bin Weevil! Pick up your trusty shotgun and blast away at some Mulch as it hurtles through the sky. It starts off easy, but it gets a lot harder – soon the Mulch will be flying thick and fast!

WHACK A WEEVIL

The evil weevils are coming! Help beat back these creepy critters before they take over the Binscape!

Use your swatter to swat the evil weevils as they appear in the holes. The more baddies you hit, the more points you'll score. Hurry, before your time runs out!

You'll score ten points each time you hit an evil weevil, and a whopping fifty points if you whack the special golden weevil. Watch out for Kip, though! He was having a nap and sleepwalked into trouble. If you hit poor Kip, you'll lose forty points!

You can find Whack a Weevil on the grounds of Flem Manor.

MULCH ISLAND

For Bin Weevils who want to get away from it all, Rum's Airport is the right destination. Step up to the check-in desk, pick up your ticket (price: FREE!), and board a plane bound for the exotic Mulch Island! From desert sands to ancient ruins, there's no telling how many secrets this island holds.

Chill out in the sand, listen to the waves and grab an ice-cold snack from the Ice Cream Machine as you bask in the sunshine with all your friends on Mulch Beach! There's never a rainy day in this party spot, so if you're feeling blue there's no better place for a break.

Sand castles and ice cream . . .
yum yum yum!

If you're in the mood to explore, Mulch Island holds many mysteries. SWS agents have been investigating some ancient ruins around the island, and hidden messages have been discovered by those who dig . . . There's much more here than meets the eye, but it will take cleverness and puzzle-solving skills to unlock the island's secrets. So keep your eyes peeled for unusual artefacts and archaeological sites!

SECRET
SWS
WEEVIL SERVICE

TINK'S BLOCKS

Why not begin your visit with a game of Tink's Blocks!

How to play: When blocks of the same colour are touching, click on one to make them all disappear. You can click on the arrows to rotate the board ninety degrees in either direction – this will make all the blocks fall down to the bottom.

TOP TIP
Don't leave single blocks of one colour behind – you'll never be able to get rid of them!

WISH YOU WERE HERE?

Hello Tink and Clott,

Greetings from Mulch Island. I came, I saw, I built a bridge! Well, I haven't built it yet, but I've found the perfect spot for the Rigg Super-Giant Suspension Bridge. Are you taking good care of my building site? Whatever you do, don't press the red button on the cement mixer!

See you soon,

Rigg

Tink and Clott
C/O Tink
Very Near to Rott's
Dump
The Binscape

SWS AGENTS
ALL OVER THE BINSCAPE

TUM'S DINER

Now that you're back from your holiday, you're probably craving some good honest weevily nosh. Tum runs this place with the help of her unglamorous assistant Slum, but her dream is to be a TV chef. Pull up a seat, or put on an apron and lend a hand – they could always use one!

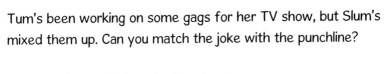

Tum's been working on some gags for her TV show, but Slum's mixed them up. Can you match the joke with the punchline?

1. What do you find on tiny beaches?
2. What's a vampire's least favourite food?
3. What did the astronaut eat his dinner from?
4. What's white and fluffy and lives in the rainforest?
5. What vegetable do you never want to find in a boat?

D. Microwaves!

C. Steak!

E. A meringue-utan!

B. A leek!

A. A satellite dish!

THE HAGGLE HUT

GONG'S PIPENEST
Make your way to Gong's Pipenest, where you can enter competitions to win awesome prizes, or pay a visit to Nab's Haggle Hut and sell your unwanted stuff!

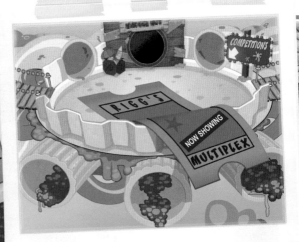

Gong's Pipenest

THE HAGGLE HUT
Selling unwanted items at the Haggle Hut is a quick way to top up your Mulch reserves. But beware of Nab's tricks when you're making a deal!

MEET THE BIN WEEVILS

NAB

Strapped for Mulch? Then Nab's the Bin Weevil you want to find. He runs the Haggle Hut at Gong's Pipenest and is always ready and willing to buy your unwanted nest items and strike a 'good bargain' (good for him, of course!). He'll even let you play a game to earn a chance for a better deal. But beware! He's known for being a bit cheeky, so if you dare to take a chance, you could find yourself with considerably less to show for it! As Nab always likes to say, 'Finders keepers!'.

Greatest ambition:

To outwit Tink and Clott.

Best moment: When he stole one of Tink and Clott's jobs.

TINK'S TREE

Tink's Tree is a magical area where Bin Weevils can cooperate to make great things happen!

By feeding flies to the tree's roots, you can help Tink's Tree to blossom and fruit.

First, you'll need to climb into the canopy to activate the yellow fly nest. Use the mushroom steps and branches to get there.

Once you've found the fly nest, the flies will be buzzing around and looking for something sweet.

Back on the ground, you'll have to scent your Bin Weevil with a Scent Flower to attract the flies, which will begin to circle around your Bin Weevil's head.

Move closer to the tree's feeding roots and the tree will gobble up the flies, helping the fruit to grow.

 Continue to feed the tree until it finally blossoms and bears fruit! When the fruit is ripe, the tree will drop seeds that Bin Tycoons can collect.

 Quick, quick! Pick up the seeds before they're gone and plant them in your garden to see what blooms.

Inside Tink's Tree you'll find another way up!

All the seeds look exactly the same, but you'll be surprised at what they might turn into . . .

Scent Flower	Step Mushroom	Tink's Tree

TYCOON ISLAND

Wealthy Bin Weevils come to Tycoon Island to get away from the masses. Here you'll find the right crowd, and no crowding. You can tell it's exclusive as soon as you see the gold-plated helicopter parked outside! Relax with the jet set or go on a spending spree in the luxury shops of Tycoon Plaza.

TOP SECRET!
Click on all the windows of the Tycoon Restaurant to light them up and see what happens . . .

TYCOON TV TOWERS

Watch cool cartoons and TV shows in the exclusive Bin Tycoon cinema at Tycoon TV Towers! Join your buddies and watch together to make it twice as fun!

If you prefer a night in, invite your friends to your nest and chill out in your home cinema room, where you can enjoy a show with pals in custom-decorated luxury. Decorate your cinema room with everything from comfy cushions to snazzy speakers!

Home cinema

THE SLIME POOL

The Slime Pool is THE place for Tycoons to hang out. Whizz down a water slide into a huge bath of slime, or chill with your buddies at the poolside with a refreshing drink while the band plays laid-back tropical grooves.

TOP TIP
To get down quickly you can also use the trampolines floating in the Slime Pool!

Oh dear! Kip has been sleepwalking again. Which pipe slide did Kip accidentally tumble down?

THE SMOOTHIE SHACK

SMOOTHIE SHACK
PLAY GAME

You can earn some extra Mulch by making smoothies for thirsty Bin Weevils in the Smoothie Shack game, or make some music of your own at the Jam Stand instead.

The price of each smoothie is the cost of all its ingredients added together. Can you work out the cost of each ingredient on its own?

 Peach on the Beach = 10 Mulch

 Lime Slime = 13 Mulch

 **Groovie Smoothie = 13 Mulch**

Awesome Poursome = 12 Mulch

119

TYCOON PLAZA

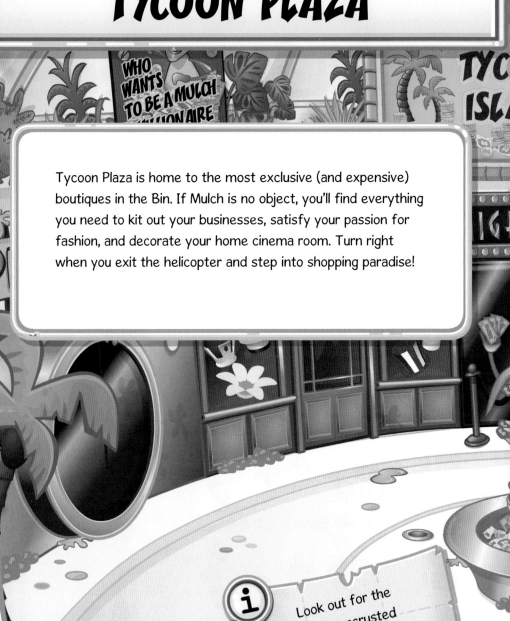

Tycoon Plaza is home to the most exclusive (and expensive) boutiques in the Bin. If Mulch is no object, you'll find everything you need to kit out your businesses, satisfy your passion for fashion, and decorate your home cinema room. Turn right when you exit the helicopter and step into shopping paradise!

Look out for the Mulch-encrusted statue of Dosh! He's a huge inspiration to up-and-coming Tycoons and the fabulously wealthy!

Quote:

'Are you still wearing that, darling?'

HEM

Hem is to fashion what fashion is to fashion. Bin Weevils' fashions change every fifteen minutes, so Hem is constantly bombarding Scribbles to write about her latest designer hats in WEEVIL WEEKLY. If she isn't busy sketching a design for some new headwear, she's out and about modelling it! Hem believes in always looking her best, and she keeps her shop stocked with everything you need to make a real weevily fashion statement! From the sweet and stylish to the weird and wacky, Hem's got the hat for you. One minute you can sport an impressive jewelled crown, the next you could be right at home in Lab's Lab with the Lightbulb Helmet.

Best momen
Opening her
Hat Shop on
Tycoon Islan

Greatest ambition:
To be named the most fashionable Bin Weevil.

HEM'S HATS

MEET THE BIN WEEVILS

BUNTY

Greatest ambition:

To collect the autograph of every Bin celebrity.

Quote:

'Oh my gosh, have you heard the latest?'

Bunty is a Bin Weevil who just loves to know what's going on. If there's some gossip going round the Bin, Bunty is sure to know about it – she might well have started it! Bunty is a loyal reader of WEEVIL WEEKLY, so she can pass on all the tastiest stories to her friends. She also loves celebrities, and she's always hanging out backstage at Tycoon TV Towers, trying to get autographs. There's no such thing as a quick chat with Bunty. In fact, Hem rang her last Friday and we hear that Bunty still hasn't hung up the phone!

Best moment:
Getting her first backstage pass.

THE TYCOON SHOP

Surround yourself with epic sound!

Admire it while watching BWTV!

BW TV

Get comfy, sit back and enjoy the show!

CLOTT'S GARDEN PLOTS

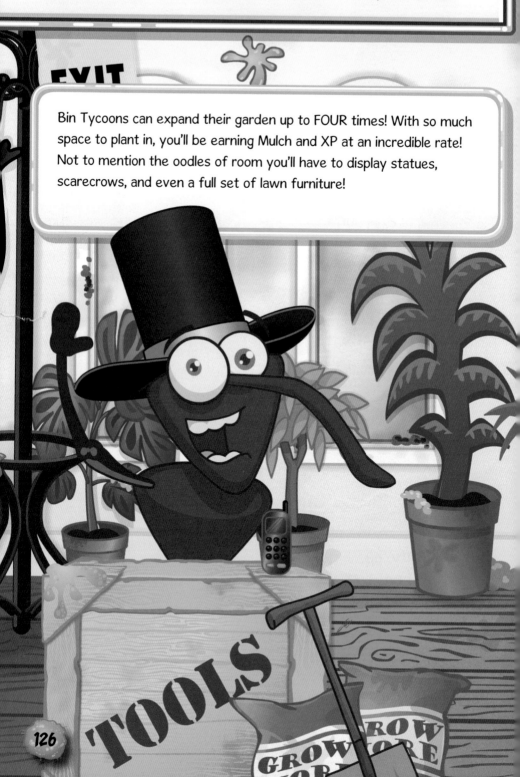

EXIT

Bin Tycoons can expand their garden up to FOUR times! With so much space to plant in, you'll be earning Mulch and XP at an incredible rate! Not to mention the oodles of room you'll have to display statues, scarecrows, and even a full set of lawn furniture!

TOOLS

GROW MORE

Super Deluxe Garden

Deluxe Garden

Larger Garden

127

MEET THE BIN WEEVILS

Quote:
'Say cheese!'

SNAPPY

Greatest ambition:
To open a photo gallery in Flem Manor.

Snappy is the Bin's photography expert. She's got the best advice and all the best backdrops to make your Photo Studio as successful as can be! Snappy can seldom be found without a camera in hand, and she loves a mag that's packed with great photos. But we'll let you in on a little secret: Snappy is actually super shy and hates to have her photo taken! She prefers to be behind the lens rather than in front of it. You can find Snappy in her Photo Studio shop on Tycoon Island.

Best moment:
When her idea for the Bin Tycoon Photo Studio was introduced to the Bin.

THE PHOTO SHOP

Spookify your photo set for Halloween!

Get right into that Yuletide spirit!

Fun in the sun is never far away!

THE NIGHTCLUB SHOP

Fling's Nightclub Shop is the place to be when you're ready to kit out your new club. From neon lights to a glittering dance floor, Fling has all you need to make your business catch everyone's weevily eye!

Chill out here and rock those tunes!
Won't wear out with non-stop dancing!
Refreshments are at hand in a cool club!

YOUR TYCOON PLAZA

Bin Weevils can access your Tycoon Plaza through the button on the floor in your nest, so the more people you invite to your nest, the more visitors you'll get to your plaza. Your plaza can also be found by clicking on your name in the Tycoon Directory (in the top hat in front of the Shopping Mall).

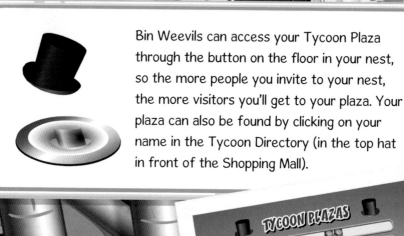

List of Bin Weevil businesses

Whenever Bin Weevils enter your businesses or buy a picture from your Photo Studio, you'll earn Mulch! To see how much Mulch you've earned, collect it from the cash machine in Rigg's Multiplex.

MONSTA STOM

You can buy new nightclub fronts and decorate your Tycoon Plaza, just like you do in your nest.

i

If you want to be listed in the Tycoon Directory so that other users can see your name in the top hat, remember to open your plaza each time you log in! To open your plaza, click on the red lock on the right hand side. It'll turn to green, and voila! You're open for business!

YOUR NIGHTCLUB

Make your club the perfect place to party all day and all night! Pick out the coolest furniture, lights, speakers, dance floor and decorations, then spin the best dance tracks to make your club the place to be! Don't forget to take out your Tycoon Camera and snap some pics of the VIPs for your magazine – all your guests will love the limelight!

Earn Mulch when other Bin Weevils spend time in your nightclub! You can collect this from the cash machine.

My friends love to party!

Keep fit by moving to the groove!

YOUR PHOTO STUDIO

Decorate your photo studio with exotic backdrops or seasonal props! The better your set, the more Bin Weevils will want their picture taken in your studio. Whenever your plaza is open or you invite guests to your nest, your studio will be accessible to anyone who wants a snapshot. Only you can change the backdrop, though, so keep things fresh with some fun accessories and invite everyone to be a shutterbug!

Earn Mulch when other Bin Weevils purchase pics from your studio! Mulch earned can be collected from the cash machine.

Bin Weevils at work!

Happy Chinese New Year!

WHICH BIN WEEVIL ARE YOU?

WHICH WEEVIL ARE YOU?
STARTING AT NUMBER ONE,
ANSWER THE QUESTIONS
AND SEE WHO YOU'D BE IN
THE BIN!

4
Do you love to know everything that's going on?
I just love getting all the gossip!
Go to 3
I don't usually know what day it is . . .
Go to 10

1
Would you rather be rich or famous?
Revoltingly rich!
Go to 11
Fabulously famous!
Go to 8

5
Do you ever lose your temper?
No, I'm always calm and reasonable.
Go to 3
Sometimes things make me mad!
Go to 10

2
Are you good with money?
I'm always trying to get my hands on more.
Go to 3
I always seem to have plenty.
Go to 10

6
Are you a hard worker?
I always give 121% (that's 110% of 110%)!
Go to 3
I'd rather someone else did the hard work.
Go to 10

3
You are Bunty – you're sociable and chatty, and like nothing more than a good gossip with your friends.

7
You are Lab – you're something of a brainbox, and you always want to know more.

8

Do you have a taste for the finer things in life?

Caviar and silk sheets all the way please!
Go to 17

I don't need fancy things to be happy.
Go to 5

13

You are Tink – you've always got a cunning plan, and a buddy to help you make it happen.

9

Do you like being the centre of attention?

Yes! Everyone, look at me!
Go to 2

I'm happy to take a back seat.
Go to 14

14

Do you like taking orders?

I'm happy to do what I'm told.
Go to 10

Nobody pushes me around!
Go to 12

10

You are Clott – honest and loyal, you're always happy to help your friends.

15

Are you good at remembering facts?

Yes, I store them in my 100 bilion brain cells!
Go to 7

I'm always forgetting erm . . . things.
Go to 13

11

Which school subject do you prefer?

Clever stuff like maths and science.
Go to 6

Active stuff like games and drama.
Go to 9

16

You are Dosh – a born leader with a taste for the finer things in life.

12

You are Rott – you speak your mind, and you're not afraid to stand up for yourself!

17

Are you good at coming up with ideas?

Yes. In fact, I've just had one now!
Go to 15

I'm not really an ideas person.
Go to 4

ALL ABOUT YOU

Favourite
trophy

Bin Weevil name:

Date you joined Bin Weevils:

Date you became a Bin Tycoon:

Best moment:

Bin Pet's name:

Magazine name:

Famous Bin Weevil you'd most like to meet:

IN THE BIN

Favourite place to hang out:

Favourite Bin party:

Favourite game:

Favourite shop:

Favourite Brain Strain subject:

YOUR WEEVILY LOOKS

Draw some of the weevily looks you've sported! Changing your
look is easy – just visit the Bin Weevil Changer at Dosh's Palace!

MORE ABOUT YOU

YOUR BIN NEST

Favourite nest items:

1

2

3

4

5

Favourite plants:

1

2

3

Favourite hats:

1

2

3

Which SWS missions have you completed?

Toughest mission:

Favourite SWS reward:

YOUR BIN BUDDIES

Draw two of your best Bin buddies and record some of their vital stats!

Fave place in the Bin:

Fave thing to do together:

Fave thing about this buddy:

Bin buddy name:

Fave place in the Bin:

Fave thing to do together:

Fave thing about this buddy:

Bin buddy name:

BIN TASK CHECKLIST

BEGINNER

Visit the Shopping Mall ☐

Purchase some nest items ☐

Decorate your nest room ☐

Find the Daily Golden Crown ☐

Play Konnect Mulch ☐

Watch a Bin Weevils cartoon ☐

Race at Dirt Valley ☐

Plant some seeds in your garden ☐

Harvest your plants for Mulch and XP ☐

Add a Bin buddy ☐

Invite someone to visit your nest ☐

Rate another Bin Weevil's nest ☐

Play Tink's Blocks ☐

Complete a crossword or wordsearch ☐

Reach Level 10 ☐

INTERMEDIATE

Buy a rare item from the Shopping Mall ☐

Buy a rare seed from the Garden Shop ☐

Adopt a Bin Pet ☐

Change your Bin Weevil's look at Dosh's Palace ☐

Help grow the mushrooms at Flum's Fountain ☐

Decorate and open your own nightclub ☐

Decorate and open your own photo studio ☐

Join the SWS and complete your first mission ☐

Earn a trophy from the Nest Inspector ☐

Help Tink's Tree blossom and collect a seed ☐

Create and publish your own magazine ☐

Reach Level 20 ☐

EXPERT

Get on the cover of another Bin Weevil's magazine ☐

Grab a rare seed from Tink's Tree ☐

Become the Top Racer of the Day at Dirt Valley ☐

Have your nest featured in BEST NEST magazine ☐

Take a picture of Scribbles or another famous Bin Weevil ☐

Buy a rare hat from Hem's Hat Shop ☐

Reach Level 40 ☐

THE WEEVILY ZODIAC

Aries (Mar 21–Apr 19)

Aries Bin Weevils like to get things done, and they're always on the move. From playing multiplayer games to zooming around the racetrack at Dirt Valley, they're going somewhere and they're going there fast! Aries Bin Weevils have loads of friends, but they're hard to keep up with because they're just sooooo busy! Aries are born leaders, so you're likely to find them coordinating an effort to get the XP meters filled at Club Fling.

Taurus (Apr 20–May 20)

Stubborn but extremely patient, a Taurus Bin Weevil is willing to save for ages to accumulate enough Mulch for that ultra-luxurious nest item. A loyal and trustworthy friend, Taurus can often be found in social areas like Flum's Fountain or Castle Gam. Taurus Bin Weevils make great SWS agents, with their careful thinking and excellent puzzle-solving skills!

Gemini (May 21–Jun 20)

Gemini Bin Weevils have the 'gift of the gab', so you can be sure to find them chat-chat-chatting! They love to learn and explore, so if they're not off completing the latest mission, you might find them taking their Bin Pet for a walk to see what's what in the Binscape. Geminis love change, so the Bin Weevil Changer at Dosh's Palace is one of their favourite places to be seen.

Cancer (Jun 21–Jul 22)

Cancer Bin Weevils have great communication skills. They love making new mags and working on word puzzles in Flem Manor. Resourceful and inventive, they like to collect lots of interesting nest items and find creative ways to display them. Don't be surprised if they make it into the pages of BEST NEST magazine by impressing the Nest Inspector with their ideas.

Leo (Jul 23–Aug 22)

Leo Bin Weevils love to be the centre of attention. You can usually find them right in the middle of whatever's happening in the Binscape, eager to be the first in line to check out parties and activities. Leo Bin Weevils are all about looking their best, so you're more than likely to spot them browsing around Hem's Hat Shop for the biggest, boldest, craziest hats and crowns!

Virgo (Aug 23–Sep 22)

Organized and helpful, Virgo Bin Weevils are excellent friends. Always ready to lend a helping hand, they love to cooperate on missions or join a buddy for a round of games. Their Bin Nests are meticulously neat, and they're known for planning out their rooms to the last detail. When they're not hanging with their pals, you can find them in the Shopping Mall, checking back for that perfect item.

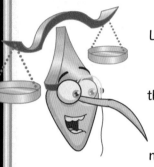

Libra (Sep 23–Oct 22)

Libra Bin Weevils love everything that's beautiful and green. They love the outdoors, and tending to their Bin Garden is one of their favourite things to do – spotting a rare seed in the Garden Shop always makes their day. Libras can seem quiet and a little bit reserved when you first meet them, but if you take time to make friends with them, they'll definitely stay your loyal buddies forever!

Scorpio (Oct 23–Nov 21)

Scorpios are brave and courageous, which is why so many of them have impressed the SWS with their performance on top-secret missions. Active and excitable, you can find them performing crazy special moves at Flum's Fountain or hitting the dance floor at Club Fling. They're also keen racers, so look out for them speeding around the tracks at Dirt Valley.

Sagittarius (Nov 22–Dec 21)

Sagittarians are known for wanting more, more, more! Their quest to level up is never-ending, and they sure know how to apply themselves to the task. They live for earning XP, harvesting their garden regularly and playing all the games they can lay their weevily hands on. As a result of their hard work, their Bin Nests are absolutely spectacular, and their nest scores are off the charts.

Capricorn (Dec 22–Jan 19)

Capricorns are playful and fun-loving. Always looking on the bright side of things, they'll surely cheer up a friend who's feeling blue. Skilled in problem-solving and strategy, they excel at games like Flip Mulch and Squares, but they're so darned nice that they might just let you win once in a while. Capricorn Bin Weevils are excellent Bin Pet owners. Their pets are well cared for and can do the craziest tricks!

Aquarius (Jan 20–Feb 18)

Aquarius Bin Weevils love to explore. You can bet they've wandered through every nook and cranny in the Binscape, and if there are hidden secrets to be uncovered, they are quickly on the case. Outgoing and friendly, Aquarians love to meet new buddies. One of their favourite pastimes is helping to unleash the Mulch catapult at Castle Gam, especially because they can chat while they're doing it!

Pisces (Feb 19–Mar 20)

Pisceans love water, and so these Bin Weevils especially love to visit Mulch Island. On the beach, they can listen to the waves lapping while they enjoy a cold ice cream. They're also really creative, so their magazines are bound to be an exciting read. Pisces Bin Weevils believe strongly in the power of luck, so they never forget to collect their daily Mulch-Tastic ticket, and they enter every competition.

LET'S MAKE A DEAL

Make a deal with your parent(s) to get Bin Tycoon membership! Offer to help out a little more around the house or do some extra chores to make them happy. Don't pester them, but show them how responsible you are and they just might make you a Bin Tycoon!

Here are some ideas to start you off:

- Clean up your room
- Make your bed in the morning
- Make breakfast for your family
- Do the dusting
- Do the vacuuming
- Help with the laundry
- Fill or empty the dishwasher
- Wash the dishes

- Watch your little brother/sister
- Help with the shopping
- Help out in the garden
- Take out the rubbish
- Feed or walk the family pet
- Wash the car
- Lay the table for dinner
- Clean up the kitchen after dinner

I, _____ (your name)

promise to complete the following chores and responsibilities for _____ (length of time) to earn Bin Tycoon membership on Bin Weevils!

WHAT I WILL DO	WHEN I WILL DO IT
Lay the table for dinner	Every day at 6 p.m.

_____

Your signature

Membership is available in one-month, six-month and twelve-month instalments. Turn to page 16 to learn more about becoming a Bin Tycoon.

FABULOUS FAN ART

boyszzz2

Emilythebrawler

Coolpiggy

153

HOW TO DRAW A BIN WEEVIL

1

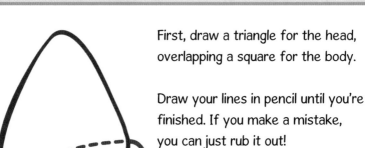

First, draw a triangle for the head, overlapping a square for the body.

Draw your lines in pencil until you're finished. If you make a mistake, you can just rub it out!

2

Now draw a line down and across the middle of the head. This will help you draw the eyes and nose. The eyes are two circles, one slightly smaller than the other. For the nose draw two sausage shapes.

3

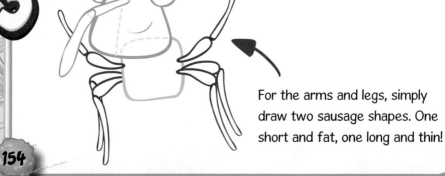

For the arms and legs, simply draw two sausage shapes. One short and fat, one long and thin!

154

4

The hands are two circles and a sausage for the thumb. Draw an outline around the shapes to make the hand.

Next, draw six squashed circles. These are the elbows and knees of your Bin Weevil.

5

To finish your Bin Weevil, simply draw over your pencil lines in the colour of your choice.

Now that you can draw this Bin Weevil, why not try designing your own Bin Weevil?

INVITE A FRIEND

1 FRIEND

5 FRIENDS

3 FRIENDS

2 FRIENDS

Have you got some friends who might enjoy Bin Weevils? Invite your friends to join the fun, and you could transform your nest into an undersea paradise with your very own floor-to-ceiling AQUARIUM!

HIP   INVITE A FRIEND   WHAT

Click on INVITE A FRIEND at the top of the page (you must be logged in to see it) and let all your pals know about the fun you're having in the Binscape!

6 FRIENDS

4 FRIENDS

7 FRIENDS

8 FRIENDS

9 FRIENDS

When your first friend accepts your invitation and joins Bin Weevils, you will get an Aquarium item for FREE and your friend will get 1000 extra Mulch. The more friends you invite, the more critters you can earn for your Aquarium. Fill your Aquarium with crazy creatures, fish and fun stuff and welcome new buddies to the Bin!

ANSWERS

EXCLUSIVE NEST ITEM!

Get an exclusive nest item by gathering the following info from this book to reveal a secret code! Enter your code into the Mystery Code Machine in front of Lab's Lab to claim your surprise.

1. What is the first letter of the Nest Inspector's last tip on his Nest Checklist?
2. How many times does the letter i appear in Lab's Best Moment?
3. How many Top Tips are there in this book?
4. How many Pea Pods are on the Pea Plant in the garden on page 24?
5. Nab's Greatest Ambition is to _____ Tink and Clott.

Put all your answers together to reveal your secret code!

1._____   2._____   3._____   4._____   5._____

Page 66-67: FIGG'S CAFE:
SCONE, DOUGHNUT, SANDWICH, MOUSSE, MERINGUE.

Page 74-76: THE DAILY BRAIN STRAIN:

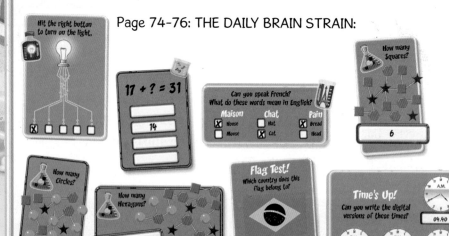

Page 79: SPOT THE DIFFERENCE!:

Did you spot the ten differences in HEM'S HATS? They are circled in this photo.

Page 80-81: WORD PUZZLES:

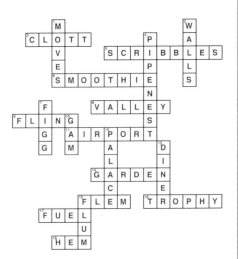

Page 107: TUM'S DINER: 1 D; 2 C; 3 A; 4 E; 5 B.

Page 117: THE SLIME POOL: Pipe A.

Page 119: THE SMOOTHIE SHACK:

 **5**  **4**  **3**

Goodbye!

That's it from us . . .
until the next book . . .
Fall in, flip out, and see you in the Bin!

Scribbles